I'M WITH MY MOM TODAY

By Angela C. Lubbe

Illustrated by Melanie Smith

I'm With My Mom Today

Copyright © 2013 by Angela C. Lubbe

Published by Lucid Books in Brenham, TX.

www.LucidBooks.net

First Printing 2013

ISBN-13: 978-1-935909-79-8
ISBN-10: 1935909797

Special Sales: Most Lucid Books titles are available in special quantity discounts. Custom imprinting or excerpting can also be done to fit special needs. Contact Lucid Books at info@lucidbooks.net.

This book is dedicated to my husband, Greg, who is supporting me through my journey of being an author, a wife and a step mom.

It is Sunday morning and Melissa is with her dad this weekend.

Bill and Mary are Melissa's parents. Melissa is five years old and loves to play with her Barbie dolls. Melissa is a lucky girl because she has two sets of parents. You see, her parents, Bill and Mary, are divorced. This means that her parents are no longer married and do not live together in the same house.

Both Bill and Mary want to spend time with Melissa. Therefore, Melissa lives with her mom on Monday, Tuesday and Wednesday of each week. She lives with her dad on Thursday and Friday of each week. Melissa is with her mom every other weekend.

Melissa is having a hard time finding something to wear to church today. Melissa peeks her head into the hallway and says, "Jan, can you come help me pick out something to wear to church?" Jan is Melissa's step mom. Bill, Melissa's dad, met Jan at church over a year ago. Bill and Jan are married now.

4

Jan replies, "Yes, I can help you. It is going to be hot today so wear something that will keep you cool." They all got ready and went to church.

After church they went out to eat for lunch and then went home to enjoy the rest of the day.

6

The next morning it was time for Melissa to go to her mom's for a few days. Bill knew he would miss Melissa but also knew that it was important for her to spend time with her mom.

Melissa has been going back and forth between her mom's house and her dad's house for two years.

It is Monday morning and this morning was special because Melissa's parents were signing her up to begin elementary school. Mary, Melissa's mother, is meeting Bill and Jan at the school to fill out all of the paperwork for Melissa to begin Kindergarten.

They arrive at the school and Melissa is excited to see her mom. Mary says excitedly, "Hi Melissa, how are you?" Melissa runs to her to give her mom a great big hug.

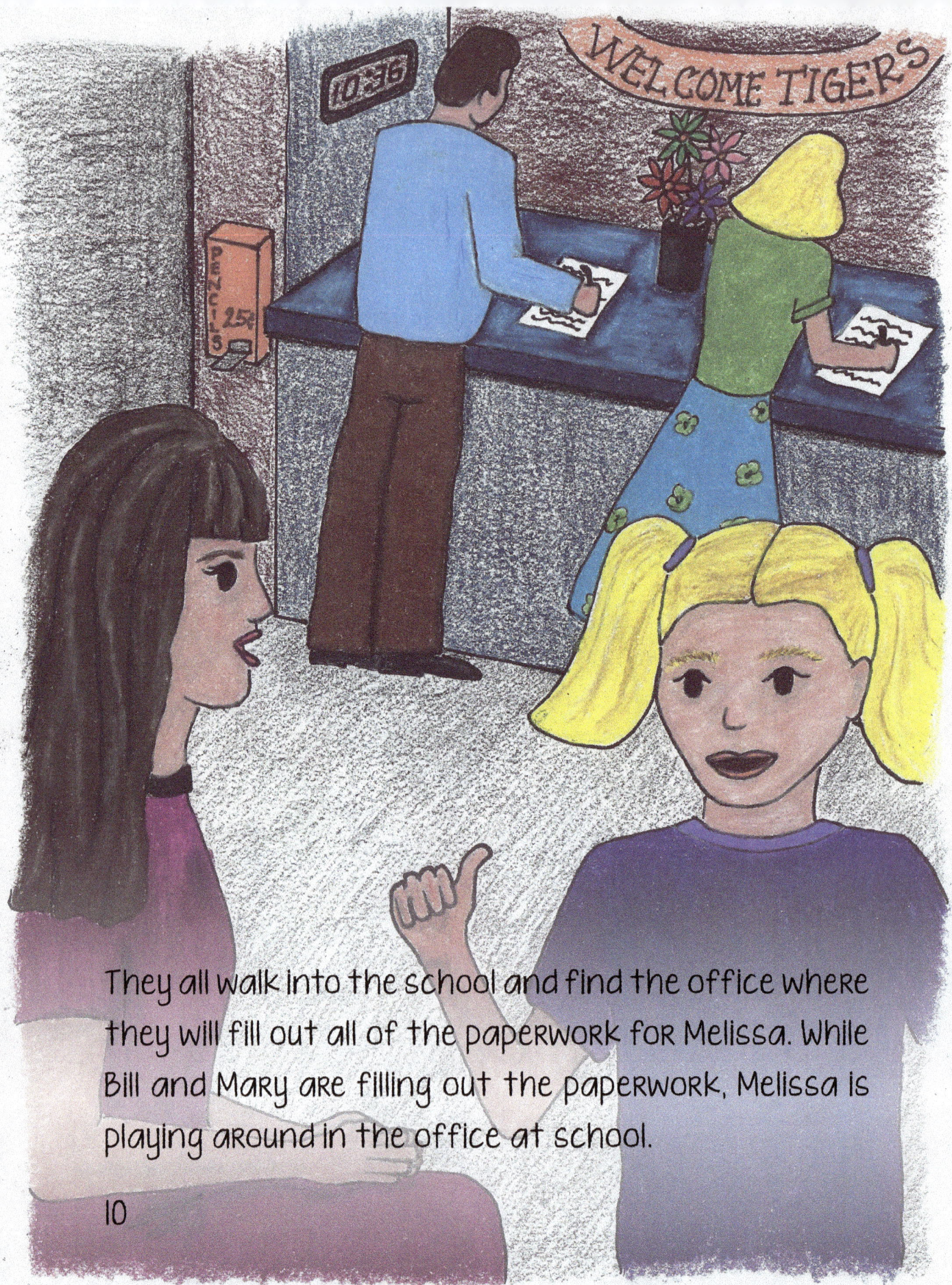

They all walk into the school and find the office where they will fill out all of the paperwork for Melissa. While Bill and Mary are filling out the paperwork, Melissa is playing around in the office at school.

Jan, Melissa's step mom, says "Melissa, please be careful and don't run around. You might hurt yourself." Melissa stops and looks at Jan and says, "I'm with my mom today."

Jan thinks for a minute and realizes why Melissa would say something like that. Melissa thinks the time with her mom and the time with her dad is a schedule. Melissa's schedule said that today was Monday and she was with her mom. It is hard for Melissa to understand that even though she is with her mom today, it is okay that Jan watches out for her safety.

After Mary and Bill completed all of the paperwork at the school, Melissa went home with her mom. When they got home, Melissa asked her mom, "Why did Jan tell me what to do today at school? I am with you today."

Mary replied, "Jan is your step mom. She is going to help you and make sure you are safe. Jan cares for you and would not want anything bad to happen to you. Even though I was there, it was okay that Jan made sure you were safe."

13

"Okay, mom," said Melissa. "I really like her. She plays Barbies with me a lot."

"I am glad," said Mary.

PARENTS PAGE

With children of divorce, it is easy for children to be confused, especially at a young age. They do not understand what is going on as much as we do. In this situation, Melissa only knows the days at either parent's house as a schedule. Children are often not sure how to act when both sets of parents are in the same room. The best thing to do is to allow the child to ask questions. Also, be sure the child feels comfortable in the presence of both sets of parents. Ask the child questions about a situation where both sets of parents were there. Give the child many opportunities to ask questions. Don't give up after one attempt of seeing if they have thoughts or concerns. It is important to let them know that both sets of parents are there to help them through any situation.